AND IF YOU DON'T GO CRAZY
I'LL MEET YOU HERE TOMORROW

AND IF YOU DON'T GO CRAZY I'LL

UGLY DUCKLING PRESSE

MEET YOU HERE TOMORROW

FILIP MARINOVICH

BROOKLYN, 2011

AND IF YOU DON'T GO CRAZY I'LL MEET YOU HERE TOMORROW
COPYRIGHT 2011 BY FILIP MARINOVICH

FIRST EDITION, 2011
UGLY DUCKLING PRESSE, 232 THIRD STREET, BROOKLYN, NY 11215
WWW.UGLYDUCKLINGPRESSE.ORG

DISTRIBUTED TO THE TRADE BY SMALL PRESS DISTRIBUTION, BERKELEY, CA
WWW.SPDBOOKS.ORG

LIBRARY OF CONGRESS CATALOGING-IN-PUBLICATION DATA

    Marinovich, Filip (b.1975)
    And if you don't go crazy I'll meet you here tomorrow / Filip
    Marinovich. — 1st ed.
        p. cm.
    ISBN 978-1-933254-80-7 (pbk. : alk. paper)
    I. Title.
    PS3613.A7487A79 2011
    811'.6—dc22
                    2010051408

PRINTED IN THE USA BY MCNAUGHTON AND GUNN ON FSC-CERTIFIED,
ACID-FREE PAPER. EDITION OF 1250.

COVER ART BY FILIP MARINOVICH. DESIGN BY DON'T LOOK NOW.
TYPESET IN PERPETUA.

FOR SEEHORSE

NO WORDS
You are right, Seehorse
Now we are a sangha

ACKNOWLEDGMENTS

Thank you to all the poets, friends and teachers who inspired, read, and listened to parts of this work as it evolved: Yelena Gluzman, Elizabeth Reddin, Ellie Ga, Marisol Limon Martinez, Ryan Haley, Guillermo Juan Parra, Jeffrey Joe Nelson, Jed Shahar, Jesse Kiendl, Greg Ford, Nathaniel Farrell, Alice Notley, Eileen Myles, Sparrow, Michael Golston, Bob Holman, Frank Lima, Timothy Donnelly, Marjorie Welish, Eddie Berrigan, Jess Fiorini, Chris Martin, Brenda Iijima, Geoffrey Cruickshank-Hagenbuckle, Nathaniel Siegel, Anselm Berrigan, Karen Weiser, Stacy Szymaszek, Erica Kaufman, Corrine Fitzpatrick, John Coletti, Arlo Quint, Joanna Fuhrman, Macgregor Card, Lauren Russell, CAConrad, Frank Sherlock, Tim Peterson, Paolo Javier, Geoffrey Olsen, Ariana Reines, Jacqueline Waters, Irina Feygina, Ilya Bernstein, Greg Houser, Dora King, Vajra, Alan Bajandas, Patrick Dunagan, Cedar Sigo, Micah Ballard, Al Marinovich, Matthew Lippman, Matthew Rohrer, Steve Dalachinsky, Yuko Otomo, David Kirschenbaum, Corina Copp, Greg Purcell, Karen Lillis, Margarita Shalina, Adam Tobin, Jim Behrle, Thom Donovan, Dorothea Lasky, Jed Shahar, Roshi Pat Enkyo O'Hara, Village Zendo Sangha, and many others.

Thank you to editors who first published some of these poems: Cecilia Wu at CRITIPHORIA, Anselm Berrigan at BROOKLYN RAIL, Tim Peterson at EOAGH, Paolo Javier at 2ND AVENUE POETRY, Julien Poirier at NEW YORK NIGHTS, Jeffrey Joe Nelson at GREETINGS, Nina Shuka Klippel, Musho, and Sara Marcus at VILLAGE ZENDO JOURNAL, Paul Foster Johnson, E. Tracy Grinnell and Julian T. Brolaski at AUFGABE, Ana Bozicevic and Amy King at ESQUE. Thank you to reading series curators who generously gave me time and an audience before which to perform this work.

Thank you to Matvei Yankelevich, Anna Moschovakis, James Copeland, and everybody at Ugly Duckling Presse for their energy, friendship, and endurance.

Thank you to my parents, Nash and Lillian Marinovich, for their love, support, and immigrant moxy. Thank you to Julien Poirier for sixteen years' constant comrade poetry pleasure and instruction. Thank you to Alicia Jo Rabins for inspiring friendship, invaluable bookshaping suggestions, and chavruta spaceship conversation. Thank you to Cecilia Wu, to whom this book is dedicated, for Everything.

— FM

AND IF YOU DON'T GO CRAZY
I'LL MEET YOU HERE TOMORROW

CONTENTS

KALEMEGDAN

and you would say when we were walking Kalemegdan park
Sometimes I wonder if I'll die before we see each other again
Now you're dead and I'm alive I never thought
I would survive your death especially right after it
you couldn't come to the Serbian expat party in Paris you said
Go on without me and walked away on silver shimmering crutches
a few weeks later I find you behind a white silo shirtless
and muscular taking apart a silver machine and we walked up

the winding stair around the white silo laughing
if you're still alive I should be spending more time with you
how come nobody told me you're alive until Grandma
laughing asked Where's your Grandpa check behind the white silo
and I did and you were laughing taking apart your machine
I want to be the machine you take apart so I can stop fearing
pain and joy of seeing you in dreams and feel your flesh
but you're all ashes now in an urn in Belgrade I return to only in sleep

again again exclaiming I can't believe I came back
I promised myself I wouldn't return after your death
but there you are laughing behind the white silo
gathering me and family beside your former sick bed
and sitting us down to eat bread you won't try
gold light from your eyes better than bread I want to fast
until you come back or I come to you but hunger-striking
for immortality would be foolish I could join you faster
could I I don't think I could unless I no I won't do suicide

I'll follow you up the white silo stairway and say
I can't believe I came back to Belgrade I promised myself
I wouldn't and yet here I am on Upper West Side Manhattan
rolling on a futon under a triptych I painted of you in Central Park when you died
I want to grow pastel crayons through my fingers and do
another and another until you come back through the oils
and sit down at the table and we eat bread together
and laugh as the white silo crashes through our window

2008

AMERICA DEATH IN NEW YORK

for Julien Poirier

ACT I: NEW YORK NEW YORK NEW YORK NEW YORK NEW YORK

New New Yorkers know how to estimate the real value of their city.
Some even dream of abandoning it all and go far away.

LEAVES. You are entitled to leaves of absence in water
treatment facility. You receive a telegram telling you there is an

emergency in the future. The first step in the process is flagellation
which refers to gentle agitation of the treated water for a period of time.

It's wonderful to stink in public. The people at the table next to me
put on life-jackets as if the extra layer will protect them from my scent.

Uh-huh. The still-life starts to rot again. After a couple of days
everything becomes a desperate craving for home. And Hygeine

can hardly form an idea of the conditions in New York
while the Plague is raging. 5 (to) rage, (to) be current

almost everywhere. The wheels of the dead-carts.
How can I salute the fireflies in the shrub-tunnel without your wreath.

The fans sing songs in the street for their team. But in here
watching porno and gameshows we wash our feet.

The only joy left is in movement and I'm moving tomorrow
to outer space where I can relax and take in the crowds

and tropical birds in burnt nests. The bombed building is
our jungle gym where a long yellow tongue of

flytape hangs from a silver chandelier studded with black gumdrops.
I feel there will always be something between us, namely the Dante icon

hanging from my neck on a white wire coathanger
but as long as you're willing to bear its impression

on your white, ivy-colored body, I will be willing to carry on.
Horrified? I told you the subways are full of young guys

who died at twenty-nine. I'm twenty-nine.
Exhume them one by one. "Report to the front desk."

I'm too busy to exhume, reading Novalis, dead at twenty-nine
soon after his girlfriend Sophie. Consumption=T.B. The waves

reached my apartment. I haven't started yet and I'm influenced—Hi!—
by announcements made underground. "HIBERNATION HAS BEEN CANCELLED."

Sonny pants in the back seat, cars pass by, it is sunny today in the city.
On my way out of New York I meet the third Elizabeth at the birthday party.

New York—a ward, a last call, a national team, the biggest mission, a well drink,
a closed ride, cormorant meat, legitimacy, roof, deal, cream, raison d'etre.

"I'll suck you off if that will give you any satisfaction.
You can slip it into me from behind then," insinuatingly.

"Yes! I go the dirty route." "Hello! I see you are home.
I'm coming over now." Surprise! impatience kills you daily

while you chase your high boyfriend from the sun.
"Don't swallow it, we can play with it with our mouths

afterwards." Comrade Tempo, look! Cannibal
banquet lighting up the town, making the sky fjordlike

with a tiny boat in it. Hi Mom, the Blowjob King won
and took my throat to outer space so I could scream at God

but the baseball field burns slowly in Baghdad, the Homerun King
rounds third, slips on an oilslick and breaks his neck. This ball

player I have in mind, invented by The Word, will lie in sand, in state,
until Dr. Benway arrives to perform penisectomy with sardine can

lids. Have you ever found yourself unable to remember
the emoticon for MISERY on hearing an enemy's name. Like in CHAPTER 1

in which it is related how Monsieur Thongboss is blackmailed and
Madame André Fontaine, completely covered with rugs and turpentine,

washes her hands with Hunter's Soap, sighing: "Four more years of
Terminal Texas, the Trojan infant president." Like the guy

who worked at the pet store and then went to work in a butcher shop
tonight we asked: "Will they stop circling and bomb us already!?!"

A reunion: each of us older, slower to speak, breathe,
quicker to order drinks. "Ride the Lightning" races from outer space

and, galloping through the atmosphere, becomes a naked boy
cartwheeling to bed. Students smoking in dorm cells look up

inquisitively. What booze remains from the secret party you left
with shells in your pockets and fuses to blow yourself up with

before the suicide bomber could get to you.
Those who look to me for sensation must, I fear, repeat

the FIREBIRD psalm. In the city of New York,
of course, once you're plugged in,

the interior is the richest of the rich. "Oh, are you still there?"
It was Saturnalia on the other line mimicing the mating noises of

a splendid porpoise! "Why, it's Madame Clovis! On with the fuck. I offer my body
in Venus's place. I must be entangled in this." A young man came to life and his prick,

in Lucy's curtained-off space, was dragged out, and his body placed
in a burning mausoleum. If Time had been, like, totally respected

it would have proved a ready detective. The tickets to Venus are
so expensive this year I want to take you there.

Do you feel closer to Madame Fontaine's Establishment
or the humunculous within. CLOSER TO NEITHER ONE.

One *is* New York. Living in New York is the first and most convincing proof of
AMERICA DEATH IN NEW YORK. New York, O New York, on the confluence of

three rivers, under the very eggplant-coloured welkin! Beginning
with the individual soldier, the next link in the chain of command is

fleeing to Paris. "Bellisimo!" I yelled to Julien out the window of Hotel Bonsejour.
Julien—we got movies—chlorofluorocarbons up the nose—

drink up for a hot New York Night. "Excuse me Mr. Hat!" calls the Madame
under the sparkling marquis of Le Thé. I should've learned to play

your ribcage. Saturday night you can watch a blue and white
minivan speed down PLACE DE CLICHY and the bumper car heart,

packed with valves and auricles, honks—DING-DONG—as radioactive civillians line up
in used car-lots. Now that spring is here I will walk until all the dogshit is scraped off

my left shoe on the cobbles of Montmartre—Place DALIDA—
Chanteuse—Comidienne—1933-1987—Saturday night you can stay out all you want

but the heart is marooned on the sun, "a fabulous wicker island."
It must be the expounding sun-spots. Feeling tall, as if a glacier had nursed me,

I seek for the next café that will house me in the mist,
kumquats split open by farmhands drip. O cold Summer Night

pissing yourself in pajamas inside my beehive hair-do.
How do you reclaim the pyramid with all your car-parts locked up in it.

This sarcophagus lid hides a perfectly good Honda! Plague
parts the curtains disguised as a nurse with half a red popsicle

in her mouth. "Tomorrow change the room!" Open the car-lot
to the wolves! who pass out in the green light of

heatwave grapes. Get the smelling salts! The patient
is made to stay awake so he can feel FLAMES eating through his couch.

Just as you shared egrets with your lover in couples therapy
you will be living in close contact with men from all walks of death.

The Angel of Death choked to death supping up the white of
an under-boiled egg. William III died from his horse

stumbling over a mole-hill. I feel ready for a whole day's sightseeing
but a profusion of trees planted after The Great Fire blocks the way. "Oh how dreadful!

But thank goodness that kind of thing can't happen again."—"I hope not.
But the view is well worth the effort." And yet, of course, that's only one aspect of

New York. Numberless swans float by and breeders throw them swan-bread.
Their cries are familiar to people all over the world as they are regularly broadcast

by the BBC. So what if I cancelled your favourite channel. Enjoy
the world's most exciting bus stops, coffeeshops and snow.

YANKEE GO HOME. Apartment renovation drilling is our favorite
aleatory makeout music and the laughtrack we hear in our kitchen feeds us

its auricular end-of-day muffins. O backpacking girl
rising to catch your train, I like being in Grand Central—a dirty bomb might go off

anytime—that suits me fine! I walk into a publisher's office that reeks of
gas and flick a lighter around to see if there will be rubble. Put me in

THE LUST COLUMN. Thank you for losing me in the crowd like that
otherwise I never would've taken a crowd-bath.

Thank you for taking me out of my tourist shell
and making me glossy mussel meat on table.

Even when it's not fully erect your delicate pink cock
is my sweetheart. My master! You have no will outside of me.

This does not mean you should not ask questions.
On the contrary, a full description of procedures is followed

when "under arms" is given in Field Manual 22-5, Drill and Ceremonies:
"When reporting outdoors, the lover will move to

VARIOUS FORMS OF SPORES, PUMPING
THE ENCAPSULATED BASILISK OF THE PAST.

Just as you stepped on the secret sea urchin of the Hudson
STOP BLEEDING. PROTECT THE WOUND FROM INFECTION.

PREVENT OR TREAT SHOCK. To be effective, let the patient move
before the lights. At evening service we offered seed-cake and flying colours

to support the human body in water. A quick return to work
is the best way of gaining health and a knuckle-duster for self-defence."

Ushered into a small chamber I amused myself with this book.
We still call one who plunders shops a "shop-lifter" in a husky voice.

2005

DESCRIPTIONS AUTOMATIQUES

you snore and it is written to the meter you breathe
in your sleep getting nearer to automatic descriptions
of the rhino trampling the greenhouse in the distance

the hippo on dry land lost his river
the bow its quiver
the coyote his shiver
where is Yelena
in Tokyo and you
cannot kiss because
you smoked a cigarette
off 103rd Street
now you have street lip
how is your equipment in sleep
in her black jeans
is it "the gay gene"
you grew from
your cellphone alarm went off

and stopped
and now you sing a telegram to your death on the couch
in the ripped open Sarajevo basement theater
while killers launch shells from the surrounding hills
and if you press a shell to your ear you can hear the

explosion of an I
too small for me
somebody busted out of me

built a statue of me
Mayakovsky
snoring was never my meter
but kicking mourners at my own wake
with a twentytwoyearold yellow
shirt tied around my neck
I hung myself and shot myself
U.S. roulette
I returned as a game made for you
you thought you dissolved
the Soviet Union
the Soviet Union is dissolving in you
a time-release pill
washed down with a white and black Russian
Prince Washington
China is Fortinbras
Curtain
asbestos
Trotsky wakes and signs the Capitol hull with an icepick
plucked from his inkwell skull
was he killed in his sleep
who murders sleep
what do you grip in your sleep
a throw pillow
on a wake-up pill
the bill comes I can't pay it
I wake up the rangers applaud
nail me to a dismantled picnic table crucifix

Today in middle class
two guys talked "What are they gonna fight with glitter...?
the guy in Wyoming...what's-his-name...and Elton John sings him..."
I gave them a look and they shut up a second
and went on talking about other things
never to return to
                    Matthew Shepard
who froze to death in a field in Wyoming
crucified on a wooden fence
what is breath for if not remembering

intervening before it is done again
knowing you are one breath from the fence
you listen and your friend sleeptalks "What?" on the couch
you "make love" to him through the computer
in the archaic sense of the phrase
age-raider
you own nothing
the socks on your feet freeze
tokens thinging
Wyoming freezes in your eyeballs

2006

SANGUIS

Shunyata
       Lumen trembling
           relax
every thing already Gong
even ink gone
we wonk on

Air to Heir   Plinth Filip   come in, Airhead
Something is rotten in this age of rope
          Wake up   listen
puttering on
a grey tile bathroom floor
on the sixth floor of a hot palace
                The Yes Palace
                SANGUIS.

In Sanguipolis grows medicinal thistle wand for calming
                initiates engaged in mysteries of
                love and blood previously feared.

                This is also known as Queering the Heir
                to the throne of Melos: Plinth Filip
                wake up if you care!

—Of Nathaniel Hosannah
know I want to know
more more more more and more
Yum Yum. Suchness! Interpersonal
Epistamen pollenation process.

Down no day
when at poems
now I lie
next to Nathaniel
half a spoon—

POEM

A perfect penis
Enters my anus
Why waste
This soft pink flesh

—from the Mullet Surprise winning epic
ANAL TONGUE DARTS

Holding hands at an orange booth—
        "I'll be right with everyone!"
says the waitress at Broadway Restaurant
SERVICE WITHOUT BILE
SERVICE WITH SATORI
SERVICE WITH VICE CUBES
MELTING IN THE SELTZER OF
HER ATTENTION

KUAN YIN
GRACIAS

Bodhisattva in white robes
surfing a sea dragon
listening to every cry in the world
never leaving Earth until
every one is ferried beyond suffering
and no-suffering
on the smoking dragon's back—

After burning
a gazillion degrees
on a midwinter's re-entry
into Earth's Patmosphere
John Revelator
seats himself
at orange Naugahyde

diner booth in his cave
for dictation WAIT
B r e a t h e

Now back to play
my heart is in my rocket
it is poems by The Air of Mardis

such as "The Candour Series for the Open Field Beyond the New York Times
Comment Field"

THUS: PERFORM ACTION ALONGSIDE PROJECTUS PROSPECTUS
MANIFESTO
or diddling is the ice you slip on
"IN LION WROTH GAMES"

"My tears are not pistols!"
I yelled from the stage
you said you listened then
in the poem all sides lungs turning
gelatinous and coated with disco ball mosaic
syllables bicycling through triphammer music—

RING-RING!   with midwinter
                                                 sixth floor scents
                                                 BAD POEM ends:

"Before unmaking hate with you
I peel my sunburned skin in Heallven
throwing it into February wind
O tickertape parade skin!
Downsizing, I'll put my body into storage
and save money eating
the closet in the porridge—

Is it still too much money?
Is it done that way?"

Will everybody gone
keep questions coming
and I have to talk back to them
not be silenced into abjection drunkeness
enough of this going around the Polis

(fear)
(fear of Sanguis
transgress
with love sex paper reams
letters to Nathaniel
in sand's rhyme scheme)

This morning I
Coach Oiseau
summon'd the
Spoojybird
by this evening I
titfucking my
Loverbird
burned at my desk
my effigy flesh
ink'd pages fresh
O assgasm blessed

Do I need to please you hurt you to keep you
attracted to me
                    No I need listen only.

Where is Gymnasium Orison
Where Therapy Thanatopos
Where Sanguis Gus on the Helio-Taupe-Ukelele

Where is air's departure from earth most evident

Lap me up, thirsty, scorched, amputated for torches Tree
                                                            Tree
                                                            Tree
Lap me up with your   TONG-LIN   tongueleaves

—Gong! levees
(salty mash)
and after mass

"MAGNIFISCAT
BY CAT BENDER"
PLAYED IN KEY OF LAUREL WREATH
NOT LETHE ORAL REEF
BUT MEMORY STRONG AND WHISKEY NEAT
AND CHORDS IN THE LEAVES—

—SILENCE! I AM LEARNING, GUS SANGUINIS,
TO BE THE ROOT NOTE ECHOING
ABOVE SPROUTING GOURD SEEDS AND ROTTING MEAT

for now I'm only a bowl of milk in your shade
lapped at by snow cats
(salty, salty!)—

SILENCE THE EAR-NUT GALLERY!

COSI FAN TUTTE=ALL IS COZY

"Did you remember to pay the toll" you ask me.

There is a toll
in no home.

Though I know you're joking
what you want is a lick
what you want is not licking you
lack of it is licking you
on your two day growth face
but I'm not it
not "the lolling bridegroom"
I'm on the atoll
we make each other with our words
volcanic lava spoojings BRAVA
cooling obsidian meerkat heads
smoking daybed.
        Breathe.
           There is no Antimatter Bird
           Laying a black hole in your blood
           Lay with me now and let fear know
           I will kill your Tollbooth Troll.

           I will kiss your lips, John
           HEAD ON A CHARGER
           I SALOME
           MY HEAD ROLLS
.................................<---.................---->...............................

AND STILL I SING. KNOW IT: I KNEEL
FOR NO CROWN
        DIALTONE
            OR PENTAGON
      ONLY TO HER
OYSTER BIRTH FOAM.

FROTH FLIRT
EVER ALERT
AFRODITA MIRTH
I WISH YOU EARTH-
LINGUS IN ETERNUS WITH WORSHIPPERS
WITHOUT WARSHIP
BUT YOU ARE
        GONE BEYOND HUT, NUT, AND HURT

       YOUR WALL-LESS
           HEARTH
               MURMUR
                  HEALS
    EVEN HERE
        IN LIBERTY
           BELL ON WHEELS.

—Well bled, Old Man!
says SANGUIS GUS
but what have you to say of
your Sanguisphobia (fear of blood mud)
how it runs in your family till you faint.
Are you with taint?

—No, Gus. I'm with my love.

—The two can be at once, O Polis Specimen Venereal Oil Florid. Say:
"I lay back and die. The angels applaud." Say:
"WAKE UP, DEAD MAN."

—I will not, Gus. I am with my Love
and healthy, fearless,
tryst in Eternus
way over mountaintop
with every flop of us
carried over together
to other shore.

        Until this
we stay on earth
with no final sign
everybody boarded
GATE train yet
or possibly
ever. Yes?

"Where are our   Out   dead friends?"
        I ask you, Gus, in "Variations on Baudelaire's *MY HEART LAID BARE*"

Syphilis to AIDS
who gets paid
for germ warfare USA   (the war on Loves)
Can't we make it carfare
to get home after a party
with a stranger to make love with
without getting sick YES!

MONK CHASER
LOCO you
    know you
       chase
          folk for love
     and, blue, see
             song
          saws
            about you—
               TING! of
                    dropped
               Chimney Green
               engagement ring.

—Persephone Paul
will you survive Hades' rape and live on
in your springcoming revival?

—IF GRACE POLLENATES
MY BLOSSOM AWAITS!
IF GRACE—   GRACIAS—   YES!
amidst planetary mess—such suffering, Amida—
          yeT—yes yes yes yes yes yes yes yes
THE SAVE ALL SENTIENT BEINGS EXPRESS
NOW BOARDING!

                    —Dingdong. First lay down the tracks.

2009

PETASOS

I like to wear my Petasos (traveller's hat of Hermes, with or without wings)
when I travel. Where am I going? I would like to announce
I do not know. I want to go on a short journey
back to the Hotel Bonne Journée
or was it Bon Sejour and stay there and play
with the bodies of my two friends,
J and K. They are both alive, why do I call them
bodies? I do not know this also. Also I eat aloe plants
for lunch and my divine name is Serving Hermes
or it is a secret—guess.
Guess. I will thieve you of your spawn, Civilization,
so you will learn a lesson about
conserving the planet's natural resources. Yes?
Yes. Also I drink much water because I need it pure
to cool down my hot-head nature. Do you have a nature?
You can light a lilac soy scent candle, place it on a handheld mirror
or handheld camera lense, take a shower and find out—

To what end. To your rear end and mine, this toast, to mind-
fulness, lest mindlessness be inclined to steal the white wine
out of your head and your calm with it. This is a guess, do you
suffer from these problems—this is a guest pouring red
wine on the carpet by the fireplace in your mansion
because you asked him what he does for a living before you offered
him free hospitality. You cannot do this to a guest, it violates the
law of Zeus, protector of Guests on High, guardian of
Civilization. Gandhi was right, it would be a good idea
both Western and Eastern. And if those two could join together
clasp hands and dancing save the planet with Romance

you might hear a secret recipe for Rice Krispy Treats
intoned by a mollusk oracle inside a jetty as Atlantic crashes

down on it, Atlantic Ocean where two nuclear submarines collid-
ed this week. Supposedly no radioactivity leaked. But would they
tell if it did? Decidedly not. Why raise panic when
so much is steak, what's for dinner, the burnt end of a cow,
what did you expect, Rump Enlightenment? I feel that when
you touch my rump and say "Ah, that's what you want, yes, ass play"
covering it with both hands and language makes the heat even
intenser throughout the bodymind. But you're sick this week,
I hope you heal quickly. I wear my Petasos (Traveller's Hat of Hermes,
with or without wings) down over my left eye to shield Sun's rays

when I emerge from Underworld bearing a fantastic red
popsicle for the Gods and when they eat it they live on
immunized against death Nothing can kill the Gods and for this I love them
we are Weak Weak Weak without the belief DEMOCRACY human-shaped
is immortal in the Universe, otherwise, thinking our actions
consequenceless, we shovel garbage into rivers
the rest of our short lives. River's foaming blue hand will reach
us and snap our necks. We like when
River does it while we're coming. River
denies us this pleasure and snaps our wig shelves
for sacrificial fire and red wine libations and
incoming naked aliens kinder to guests than we ever were
when we hammered together gallows
welcoming Xenos with rope.

2009

THE GREEN HAG SPEAKS TO THE STATE

You could burn me at the stake
but with what wood
you've used up all your forests
and my forests, now safe in my mind, will exit
will march on you
climb your fortress walls
and silence you
stamping you into earth
until real forests grow again.

2009

ODE TO ALICIA JO RABINS

I. ANCIENT

Today we met
in a laundry
in a lake
in my left shoulder

now I'm inside
     a toupee filled with blood
  aping the skyline.

You taught me
Poetry—
     it's so much
to receive.

I do my laundry
on Earth.

I pretend I end
the war with a word
in a lake
with nitrogen rain.

I save the corpse of a lover
who died in the desert
fasting and praying and reading
a fossil on the underside of a stone.

Knowing that you are
an alien the shape of my hand

I want to
   fast.

What you find is an Ancient.

II. ACROSTIC

At dinner time I know you want to eat
Love's lion chops and flames beneath our feet
It gives me ecstasy to introduce
Chavruta of the spirit in the spruce
I once thought she would never travel back
And that I'd lose her to the sea and lack

Joy enough to write her when she wrote
Of tying ropes aboard a tossing sailboat

Right now I know that she is almost here
And writing her feels like raving a year
Before she comes to visit me and smiles
In her gaze quiet tomboys still go wild
No need to ask if I will court my death
Since she came back I spurn it breath by breath

III. A TRAVELLING PART

I wanted to tell you about shivering in the dust of golden arms
and for a moment was quiet about the source.
What you and I were doing before
could never equal this
and you knew it, went away
and gave up the title Poet
moved deep into the woods around
The University of Hafiz and looked
as the deer gathered and you played violin
for them until they revealed to you
their king selves for a minute
then retreated back into the trees
on the sound of footsteps in the leaves.
Ian later told me IT WAS REAL
ANIMAL-CHARMER STUFF and I believed him.
Do you? Do others' reminiscences of you as
a visionary make you blush? I'm never
there when you call this week because I'm
writing with this pen I call Hypodermic
under my rising sign—Leo—I think—or is it
Ferdinand, the prince asleep in the waves

until a spirit withdraws from its tree
to save the day. Two lemons on the toaster-
oven, one pill, one glass of water and
it's off to bed with the rest of us

who kneel when you breathe across
the Atlantic just under the Mediterranean's
polluted blue shoulder. Thank you for giving
me willpower, if such a thing can be
given. The lights are too far apart
in this apartment but when I look
for reading light you appear with
your one-eyed vases and tickle my
sex into shape as the angel did
to the baby in the manger where he lay
laughing and throwing hay high into
the air, blushing to receive such
clear instruction from Heaven's pair
of stars travelling at incredible speeds
to arrive on time to the car race
where you are the referee, wave the
flag, shoot the gun and we are off—
the taste of burnt rubber on my lips

makes me come at the wheel while
the other ejected me falls asleep in the
clouds, the one cumulus, the other storm
and I awake once more in the light blue
arms of chloroform where the surgeon
touches my genitals and tells me:
"You're alright, Kid, I've hacked up
a lot of civilians who never returned
with a pulse—Get out there and play

or your hesitation will cause
your death which can eat up a
perfect concentric circle of
trees in a minute."
                    You go on to
the next nightmare in my notebook and
check that one off and tell me to forget it.
You will dictate to me the record of
the brightest wet dreams from the century we
just lived through the end of, after which,
if we still live, you lie down next to me,
part my hair, and whisper: "You have
a travelling part." Pleased to hear this
I go to kiss you and feel my lips against

a cold matte white poetry book spine. I will
wear its indecipherable hieroglyphs on my lips until
you kiss me for real and open my mouth
again for a return commitment
to our program of eradicating coulrophobia
and teaching each other what co-muses mean
to each other through daily practice of
the scales necessary to master
conversation on the rounds we make
of the forest just outside Haifa where
the deer come up to me now too and
ask me how you are.

2002 / 2004

AT A DESK IN BELGRADE

observing words
as facts
how do they act
and interact

jam and see
not experimenting
but singing
in the highest tree
you can find
at your desk
in your findings
be clear
relentless thorough
burrow

under the tree
open your eyes and see

observing words
phenomenology
word sculptures brick by brick
and what do they suggest to your soul
sing it

observing words
as facts
how do they interact

move and see
and seeing sing
swing that thing
sweet the etherling
circus in the sphere
presence is
when You
are near
Blue
One

2006

OCTOBER 2001

You want to make love in Kandahar
with the bombs coming down.
The tradition of naming ships after
women will change because

the smart bomb misses the helicopter
by a mile, razes a village.

War is a test with no results
until you are   thin air
on a diet. But everything you know
is a soda system
                whether you dine
in the college or not. The cafeteria
opens its doors to churchgoers bloody
from dreaming Kandahar
      love in caves when bombs fall—
      that   orgasm inside the rock
another you love in the cave. A veil.

2001

LIVE FROM THE KAUKASUS

for Matvei Yankelevich

This liver feels really sharp in me,
The beak sharper.
Crafty Fileep, get out your SUV and drink its gasoline.
See how it fuels you—can you get off the Kaukasus with it?

Will your asshole become the tailpipe
To blast you off the crag you're chained to
And will this eagle fuck off already
With its lightningboltbeak—

Crafty Fileep, McPrometheus, your liver is a Big Mac
The eagle eats when it rips through your ribcage.
You are bleeding to death. Have a Q-tip. Stick it in your ear,
Pierce your eardrum, laugh and hug that eagle coffin.

2005

OBJECT RELATIVE

This object is my relative
I treat it with a sedative

When it keeps me up for fights.
Object, you are an actor corpsing on footlights

You impale yourself on.
Sharp lenses! cut through the skin of my inner alien

In my nightstand. My legs, table legs—what's the difference?
This egg before me is exactly what I feel inside.

2005

DELFT RETINA

What than this
its its
a every

through the of
No here to
through the a

of the a
into and
toward

In a in the
us of
A of out

into the of and
no of the
of Delft the the

in and over the
what a with
were here here in

2006

THE GIFT OF EAVESDROPPING

for Alice Notley

sitting on a red standpipe siamese
 a perfect place to eavesdrop
  to give the gift of eavesdropping
   but you're hunched over
    you know how everything you've done
     it doesn't work because
        you're conscious of it

And Spanish I can't understand
      let alone transcribe Why?
   Get yourself to language class
                    Lazyass

   A BODY FALLING OUT OF A CEILING
            SCREAMING
         "THAT'S GOD!
            A GUY!"

    That's true! but no potatoes

What've I been doing
with all these people in harmony with me
Sitting on a red standpipe siamese

    The eye sees what the eye gives
       "We are led to believe a lie
           when we see
               not thro' the eye"

William Blake stars
as The Tarot Reader
shuffling blue construction paper cards
at the round table
12 poets sit around
diagnosing civilization
the already gone ghost membrane pajama
Sleepwaking in it do you curl up
your sleeves and get to jerking the pen off
as the tour operator does his microphone atop the blue doubledecker
telling the Guests about SOHO
short for SO LONG HOUSING

Oh Soho!
this tomb is stone fondue
while I eavesdrop

STOP

I think I owe you
TAR spots on the street
you wouldn't necessarily be putting your
lipwear on your shoes
Houston and Broadway
SHOWER PUPPETS! two dollars each
sketching in midafternoon grey
slate of sky Daniel thank you
Off the standpipe finally and waiting for the spider to bite me

Do you want a finger puppet

Mine are all thinner
The Lovers eye The Web
　　BANK OF AMERICA spread

　　"What the function of this luncheon"
　　　a bad joke eyed eleven years ago
　　　　when I was taking Koch
　　　　　and he drew a rabbit on the board
　　　　said Go see Cy Twombly

JAIL PUPPETS!

　　We don't have enough rich words
　　　　no soil but
　　　　a concrete square
　　　with tar spit circles
　　　　on it

　　Oh train translate that
　　The shower we ran
　　　We rented out a couple
　　I've been a man for six
　　　　months already warm out
　　and now napalm
　　that's why I always
　　　　　　　CUE THE EYE.

Or do you want this guy over here

   My butt is cold from sitting on this
   red standpipe siamese

  If there was a fire
  I would've been the water gladly
  since I'm tired of playing Chutes
               and Ladders
  I can put out the flame
                    glove fitting
                    itself over
                    fire escape fist
                    pulsing

 Sepulchre Mice eye The Web Lovers
         bringing frozen pizza
home to monochrome
                   gold walls of rest junket
       REST AND LEASE

   while the real interrupts you with
coughing a little bit more
                  artistic
                  finger puppets

without interruption
　　is no thinking
　so I cough
　　through your aria

The cellphone rendering
　　　in like a basket hat
　　　telepathy relevant again
　　though weakened by constant radiation
　　　to the head and digits weak from punching
　　and Presto Digitalis where is the
　　　motherboard
Greg said I need to buy
　　　　My motherboard is broken
　　　　　What does it taste like? Everyone
　　and I can buy a new motherboard

　　Are we stopping you

The Eyeball
caught
in The Web
looks at
The Lovers
in the treehouse

YOU STOLE MY ERRAND
YOU CROWD
ROWDY WITH CONVERSATION
BUT I WAS HAPPY TO BE FREE OF IT

I CAN SEE YOU GET THE
NEWSPAPER
THROUGH A GLASS NEWSPAPER
IN MY EYE

The Web is catching up
 as it walks
behind The Lovers racing
 away from
    The Flood Card
 as it gives a long
   paper cut
  down the eye
 of The Prophet
  in the treehouse

I met five magazines
  on Spring and Prince

      Baking soda snorter
        short on calming substances
          to be shared not controlled
          Ah substances

To pick tar spots off the street and smoke them thereby
affirming intimacy with the sidewalk still here

since SoHo became buffalo marionette cut loose from phone booth

    afternoon wet cement fondue
      dip your pen in it and
        write the recipe in time
        for the cook to die
        The cook is you

    And all of this is foretelling what?
    You're just a meteorologist
      perusing bra-straps
        at Victoria's Secret
        looking for a sign in the ink
      or a pinafore
    or the pianoforte to score with
    Ah sex with an objective correlative
  finally I find the Hanged Man and

                    then they kicked
        all the people out of housing

    The Lovers find The Eyeball
            on the spiderweb
              enticing
        for the web was sewn in the wound
            of the slain toro
          in the middle of the arena
        to mark the place where the
            toreador cut its balls off
          to give to the princess
    Next time is goring time and
        comas and death and a
      game of cards played by nurses
        in the waiting room interrupted by a
    crack in the floor The glacier the
    hospital was built on opening up to say HELLO
                        WHAT TIME ARE YOU GOING HOME?

2006

AT THE CATHEDRAL OF ST JOHN THE DIVINE

I gave you cunnilingus in a dark alcove
while poets took turns reciting "The Inferno"
in the Poet's Corner. It was our turn.
My nose started to bleed while I gave it to you.
I noticed a metallic taste, I thought it was you.
I got up and wiped my finger against a note
tacked to the wall, leaving a dark streak.

We walked to the bathroom and cleaned up.
David came in and said, "Wow, Studio 54!"
like I had been taking cocaine.
It was a much more powerful drug,
your fuck.

We sat in a pew for an hour afterwards hugging and necking
and wouldn't leave when a priest strode by demonstratively.
The dark protected us, and the fact that this was a modern,
non-denominational cathedral. One of only two
authentic cathedrals in America. Well.
We were staying.

Outside a lineup of firetrucks made the cathedral front glow
red and blue. We were both concerned about AIDS
but didn't know what to say.

When we broke up it was almost your birthday.
We talked about Anna Akhmatova in Sakura Park grass,
and you translated a couple of her verses for me.

When you stayed late at a party I threw
I left "for a walk." You said you would leave
if I left. I left. You stayed. "Well, she's great,"
Julien said to me later. I couldn't agree at the time.
Now I dream you come back to me every couple of weeks
and you are simultaneous translator for a Russian theater director.

2003

WISH

I wish that someone
would come to me
in the middle of the night
and fuck me very hard
against the bedstand
so that the shriek would glow
like a magnet in my hand
and by my side would appear
friends now gone.

2000

THE MOURNERS

                  can hear light
and hear voices coming out of light
whether they want to or no
as silence leaves the world carbonated
water inside a clavichord.

2000

LIGHT AROUND A PILOT

in memory of my grandfather Milos Marinovic

I. SVETLO OKO PILOTA

pescane plaze	sand beaches
i vukovi u glagolima	and wolves in the verbs
"vucija so"	"wolf salt"
po dlanovima	on palms
domivina	home and wine
bela	white
gotova	finished
ciao	ciao
dobro vece	good evening
kako ste	how are you
ja sam	I am
Fili	Fili
znaci	meaning
Poljubac	Kiss
na Grckom	in Greek
Ziveo Ja	Long Live Me
i svi sto su me naucili	and all who taught me
sta i kako i ko i o nocnom zivotu	what and how and who and of nightlife
i o Jadranskom moru u kojem	and of Adriatic sea in which
sam plivao s njim	I swam with him
dok mi je pricao price o	while he told me tales of
Mornaru Popaju	Sailor Popeye
kako je zapusio usi	how he plugged his ears
sa vax	with wax
da nebi cuo sirene	so he wouldn't hear the sirens
i njihove pesme	and their songs

smrtonosne
koje tonu mornare i sve
i onaj ko je rekao
"Ozeni se da se ne ubijes
sam u cetiri zida"
i onaj koj vise nije
s nama
nego svuda
u plucima
u udisanju u izdisanju
Deda
Deda
Dead
Deda

deadly
sinking sailors and all
and he who said
"Get married so you don't kill yourself
alone in four walls"
and he who is no longer
with us
but everywhere
in lungs
inhaling exhaling
Deda
Deda
Dead
Deda

Alive inside
Fili meaning Kiss in Greek
He taught me Greco-Roman wrestling
his blessed release from suffering is
a diamond
shooting through paper
no perfection no breath no life
and breathing here alive
but no I won't dive on top of
the coffin
though it would be cinematic

Dead at 93 just after the full moon in Aries

The Pilot Svetlost flew down to my runway heart and landing
walked out on the wing and said
Ziveo Mi Filipe!   Long Live Filip!
I saw him flash in a star and say
WE COME TO HEAVEN AS OUR BEST SELVES
the pilot who flew when shot down by Nazis
into safe landing and survived generations of
poison   murder   interrogation
my grandfather teacher and first love Milos Marinovic.

II.

       Grampa Mercy sleeps at the bottom of
the convergence of the Danube and Sava rivers
one day to Awake

No he was cremated
So
Awake

III. "WE COME TO HEAVEN AS OUR BEST SELVES"

my grandfather woke me up at four in the morning
with a panic attack to tell me
in a white star FLASH
he'd gone—("Called Back")—
  I yelled "Deko!"
  took an Ativan
  fell asleep
later that morning
I was woken up by a rumbling on my heart
his WWII allied fighter plane
had landed on my runway heart—
I knelt and prayed before the small
golden Buddha by the lamp
and heard Grampa
standing on the wing of his plane
yell out "ZIVEO MI FILIPE!"
    "LONG LIVE FILIP!"

I didn't know if he was alive or dead and
shivering I was a shaman who might know
how to help him but I went to see a psychiatrist instead
thorough calming kind and going to Mexico
next week may the Gods bless him and his family
he gave me the meds making my mind
a well made bed again or a cot at least for now
a night ago I was growing black feathers from my arms

before the mirror a shadowy magician
with a tall slouching black top hat
on my head I pressed a dead phone to my ear
chastizing myself for not being present
at his deathbed to experience the process
would it've made it easier would I have gone even madder
if that's possible O yes
a blessed dialtone and pill-induced sleep

IV. TO ELIZABETH AND JACQUELINE

It's as if I wanted to, with perfect clarity, apprehend my grandfather's death to keep it from happening. And I went to the monastery to do it in ecstasy. I thought enlightenment could happen and then stay and no suffering though living could be. Wrong. *Gong! The life of a monk is not for me, my mind does not have that stability!* "My mind goes like this." "How does my mind go." "It goes...like that." "I like that. You should be thankful for your mind. It has a lot of pizazz. Daphne said so at the ramp to her show. Everybody who comes into contact with it says that."

"I feel like this city is fucking me in all my holes," I said to Jacqueline. She said "That's what everybody's saying," laughing, leaning against gallery glass, "but I miss it in Pittsburgh I love it in Pittsburgh yesterday I got a brown belt in karate." I said "The art of self-defense!" and she didn't hear me and I started talking about poetry teachers and nodding she replied: "Everybody says 'intention' but that's just believing somebody else's religion. All you have is the information given by your senses."

V. INSTRUMENTALITIES

Fil,

      artifact is ash
      ash is artifact

          fill your resonation chamber
          with mufflers. It's ash.

      Ash is artifact
      artifact is

          a find.
Make one. No. Gas. Oxygen. Breathe
smile write paint sing play
              ILLUMINATE.

VI.

a cork plugging up
a hole in Earth's atmosphere
popped out, rendering it
a zero gravity planet

and I'm sucked upward
and it's   him in my lungs
gives me breath to sing
remembering
every part of
my body filled
with him
here no longer

I'm him
so I better
climb in the cockpit
and take off
with lungs that can take any altitude
even the rapidly changing one
when he was shot down by Nazis
and survived the black oiljet
gushing against his lenses—

VII.

       Grampa Mercy sleeps at the bottom of
the convergence of the Danube and Sava rivers
one day to Awake

No he was cremated
So
Awake

2007

BODHISATTVA GRAPHOMANIA

ODE TO AUGUST 2007 FRIENDS
Summer Meditation Retreat—Ango at The Grail, Cornwall-on-Hudson, NY

> *"The whole of spiritual practice is good spiritual friends."*
> —*Shakyamuni Buddha*

*

TO JOSHUA MOSES AFTER DISCUSSING VARIOUS TRANSLATIONS OF THE HEART SUTRA AT "EAST-WEST BOOKS"

"Enough bookstore profundities"
what I need is
  an encouragement stick
 shoved so far up my ass
  it tickles the underside of my skull.

*

who is
 walking toward me
        while I'm sitting Zazen?

laundry in peripheral vision—
        monks'
          black and white
            robes
          blowing on

five white lines—

Where *who* is sitting Zazen?

＊

"Flying in from Toronto I was struck by how run down
Laguardia Airport is. I was like 'Oh—America.'"

"Yeah. U.S. is over. America is going down."

＊

**ROSHI'S INSTRUCTIONS TO JIKIDO ("PERSON WHO KEEPS TIME AND
CLEANS THE ZENDO") ON HOW TO USE THE MORNING WAKE-UP BELL:**

"It rings on it's own, you just walk."

＊

NOTES FROM DOGEN STUDY WITH ROSHI

"Well you know how theory is.
Theory's like looking for your keys in lamplight
'cuz it's a lit area."

*

ROSHI ("Zen master, literally 'old teacher'")
"Roshi doesn't exist
it's just energy."

*

TO MY NEW ROOMMATE

When you rushed into the room I was resting on my blue bed
you said: I DON'T KNOW WHY I'M HERE I DON'T LIKE ZEN
I DON'T LIKE THE FORM!

TRY THE EMPTINESS!
I replied and we laughed at each other
two wrecks
recognizing each other
as you unpacked a black duffle bag on your blue bed.

*

And Roshi said:
"Who am I now
who am I now
who am I now
keep asking yourself that
and if you don't go crazy

I'll meet you here tomorrow."

Who am I right now?
                OUT   IN   ARRAY

Peacock   Day,   embrace
Michelle and I as we look a long time into each other's eyes
telling each other   slowly   what we see.

      *

"When reading Dogen's UJI
('Being-Time' or 'The Time Being')
tonight remember to ask
not: 'What did he mean by this?'
but: 'What does this mean FOR ME?'"

      *

in boarding school
North Andover, Massachusetts, Earth
first time coming
tilted back in green swivel chair
behind blue locked dormroom door.

*

ORYOKI ("CEREMONIAL MEALS")

What napkin goes where
which spoon wooden when
do I cover my mouth
when I suck it to clean it

is there a nipple to suck here
to calm myself
I'm a wreck   —Be with that

"Who am I now Who am I now Who am I now
keep asking yourself that
and if you don't go crazy
see you again here tomorrow."

    *

Who are you now? looking for deer
                    in the woods behind The Grail house—

              you scared them off
            with your twigsnapping
                  feet.

*

3 wild turkeys on grey driveway hilltop
   inching toward
               backyard basketball hoop—

      Are silver and blue
           Bud Lite cans
               indigenous to this
                    upstate New York forest—

Chainsaw sound
    far up ahead.

*

incense stick breaks
when I try to stick it firm before
travel altar Manjushri with sunflowers—

"You are also the stick of
incense breaking" said Roshi and
"When Shakyamuni Buddha was enlightened
he said 'I and all sentient beings are enlightened'"

Roshi calms with her words
inviting us to discuss
UJI "THE TIME BEING" UJI
even when her tooth hurts
her Pisces smile flashing!

                    *

my grandfather, my first teacher, sick a month
now in Belgrade intensive care.

                    *

WHY DID YOU DECIDE TO COME TO STUDY WEEK?

        JUNE 21ST, 2007
the summer solstice
              the closest we tilt to the sun
and membranes and shields and
filters melt, bodies dancing, free festival music
on Manhattan streets I'm walking around "Morningside
Heights" the corporate real estate name
for Harlem Takeover and Forced Migration—
How can education take place in that
kind of karma field or does
ivy keep   karma out or
are we all hooked up to IVs and

don't know it—I'm walking to Morningside
Park, greet the solstice sun—
I turn and walk back to Riverside Park and
run into Aimee and Greg and before
that I stop at a street bookseller
and buy a book on KUAN YIN,
Bodhisattva of Compassion.

I sit down with the book and
Greg and Aimee, and Aimee asks:

"Does that work—enlightenment?"

"I don't know
              I've never been enlightened.
But meditation works."

"Yes," says Greg. "Meditation works
even if you're a beginner your whole life.
I have to go back to work now."

"Happy Solstice…bye!"

I walk down Riverside Park
   grass hill to write and sit
      and nothing's coming
 so I open the Kuan Yin book
  to read the Heart Sutra
  looking for a jump start

            I begin and get
to the word VOID in
    that translation and think back
to Philip Whalen Zenshin Ryufu Meditation Mind Imperial Influence Dragon Wind's
    (Peace be upon him)
        talk at Green Gulch Farm:

"I think there's a great deal of misunderstanding about what emptiness is,
the idea that emptiness is something that happens under a bell jar
when you exhaust all the air from it. That's not quite where it's at
as far as I understand it. The emptiness is the thing we're full of,
and everything that you're seeing here is empty.
Literally the word is shunya, something that's swollen up;
it's not, as often translated, 'void.' It's packed, it's full of everything——" and

that's the last thought I
remember having I was
in Shunyata all of it
part of it everything
participating all I trembled
panicky called on Avalokiteshvara
to protect me He did I moved
into the shade of a tree in bliss and
sat watching everything being with
everything no me there anymore
everything green green green
blue
Light
rays going out
of everything
into everything
and
OUT
again
and
again
and
goingon

walking after a while
buying 2 cookies from cookie seller girls
being in love with

everybody in the park
even the green bug I blew off
   my notebook and wanting
to make love with a man sitting on
   a hill writing in his notebook
in his black and gold
      Pittsburgh Pirates   *
         hat with the
            gold letter "P".

         *

"Everything is included:
ecstatic experience or hell realm or ordinary
experience. We all have all of those in us—our lives
are so full. Appreciate all experiences, don't just
take them for the one narrative, make them narratives
again and again—re-narrate—

Every moment is enlightenment if you can be with it,
not push it away."

                  Who am I now
                   What is this
                      at Manjushri travel altar
                   green incense stick
                                 breaking in hands

"You are the incense stick breaking.

When Shakyamuni Buddha became enlightened
        he said

    'I and all sentient beings are
                    enlightened'

    Practice *is* Enlightenment
            be practicing
                    when you practice."

Am I listening? No—planning:
                        following Zazen
learn all forms of Oryoki with Fugan
            in less than ten minutes.

            *

Fire is fire
                no segue
Ash is ash

when it's log it's log
        not future ash
    and when it's
    ash it's

ash

log burning
   each moment
            has integrity...

Roshi:
"Help me out with this you guys
it's not like I'm the guru of time!"

Rinzai:
"Right now there's a person of no rank
flowing in and out of
the holes in your face" (your senses)

it's woodchuck time
it's five of woodchuck

"When you do something great
it might be Dharma
manifesting itself in you.

Not 'self-improvement'
Dharma is still flowing through us
even if we're not in good shape
no need to believe
the story we're telling ourselves
about ourselves."

*

Grandfather fighting to live now. I pray he
lives on.

*

Time is Mala beads
sometimes one bead
sometimes a string of beads
curving

> "I'VE JUST BEEN WALKING AROUND REALLY
> FLOORED BY BLOSSOMS"

Not abacus beads side by side to count money
but a round Mala to swing

Time is
    log being log
    ash being ash

    "Being-Time"

    UJI

    THANK YOU DOGEN

KANZEON

ROSHI

*

waiting outside in a
white plastic chair
to see Roshi,
two students ahead of
me to go
      "How can I articulate my resistance
to counting breaths while sitting—
my father terrorized me with math lessons—
a hell realm—I can't count the breaths—I can—
but it makes me very nervous."

But thinking this
a tiny cool green leaf
fell onto the palm of
my active hand in Zazen mudra
I looked down and saw it
WOW   time stops no thoughts
looking up the first thought is One

one leaf
Earth
Earth
one leaf

Earth guiding me
with leaf

leaf Being
Being leaf

      covered in mud
      thinking and spattered with muddy water

    But out of
    mud-
    dy
      water
        grows the

          L

       S O

       u T

"But even the lotus has a tiny speck of

dirt on it" said Roshi.

                    *

one   leaf

            communicating

                    Relax

                you are not separate from

        suchness

                    I put the leaf into the right
                    pocket of my sweat
                    pants Thought I might
                    give it to Roshi
                    as a gift
                    hold it up like
                    Buddha delivering
                    The Flower Sutra
                    but glad Roshi
                    asked me
                    about breathing
                    practice instead,
                    advising:

"Embodied breathing:
Envision your mind
pushing your breath
down into Hara
filling your Hara

and pushing the breath back out.
Thoughts will still come
'Am I doing it right?'
'When is the bell going to ring?'
bring it back to breathing
mind pushing down and up breath."

        *

waiting to see Roshi
in 3rd chair from the front
as Earth is 3rd planet from
the sun the sun is you Roshi
in a wooden hut
seated and swaying
listening with whole body
to holes in what I'm saying.

  The way you
         s
          w
         a
          y
           e
            d
      when listening to me
       like Green Mother Tara   and   Manjushri
       on either side of

                    Shakyamuni Buddha
         in the thin frail paper mandala
            blown off the white closet door
               and taped back up
                  by sentient being me taking Klonopin to feel fixed—

         "But you're not broken
            that's a fiction.
            The core belief of
            our culture is
            we're damaged
            need fixing.
            It is a fiction"
            said Shuzen
            a bandaid tied around the left corner of
            his eyeglasses by a friend
            whose name I have forgotten—
            Thank You Friend—

               above in the trees
         a woodchuck
                        a bird
            green leaves
                           fanning out
               in full array
                           before me, with me,
                     in me
         as I'm in them

LEAF-BEING.

*

West Point
jet pilot
       practicing "maneuvers"
              above us—

       "I like that" Roshi said
       "I like that
              we are practicing so close."

       Dear Roshi,
       I can't sleep
              a green planet
                     is in me
              I want to be
                     studying
                     with you
                            right now.

*

"TOP T FLITE
TOUR RANGE"
 golf ball
  lodged in muddy grass
I am about to pick it up and don't

it might be a booby-trap
Am I acting in a Vietnam movie
    why not Iraq
"PEOPLE ARE DYING IN IRAQ
    The unsaid"
        said Roshi

                *

Walking through The Grail woods
during our afternoon break
I paused before
NO TRESPASSING
scribbling:
That's where you bow
    and cross
        and start
            your walk

    Lines
    Borders
    Markers
        porous
    Breathing beings walking
                yes
        private a lie
        property a delusion

in suchness
thusness
just now

(bow)

Tried to sleep
after first Dokusan ("Private meeting with the Abbot") with Roshi
and two Daisans ("Informal interview with a Dharma-Holder")
with Shuzen
Blessed are they
may they live long in health
and complete their vows

but I kept having delirious halfsleep dreams
of people telling me what I should do
and how to do it
in the kitchen in the Zendo
in the Buddha Hall presided over by
KANZEON
Blessed be He Great OCEANIC
BODHISATTVA COMPASSION
PRAJNA PARAMITA WISDOM
Thank you I took a Klonopin 0.5 milligrams
it almost dissolved on my tongue by the time I
got to the water to gulp it down
and my eyes sore from writing

by dim blue cellphone light
the words what words
when you sleep you sleep what happened to those
words inaccesible with Insomnia rocking
me awake in gentle hell realm
          "Bridging" comes next
as Shuzen taught me caress your left wrist
of crickets making runway noises
as all Ango participants and you
Filip Marinovich without a Dharma Name
take off, airplane-like, no, are stranded on runway
waiting to fly to the Vermillion Palace—
                              Birdsounds bring
you to now
          like when Rodney asked his wife
what was your face before you were born and instantly
she looked up said Dirt.

          *

FIRST DOKUSAN WITH ROSHI

"I liked your story very much about Riverside Park today
my concern is that you cling to that
THERE'S SO MUCH MORE
I don't want you to miss out on the subtle things

Counting is not an act of oppression

just to keep you in time

Now we're going to skip a grade

Embodied breathing
mind pushing breath down
filling your Hara
and pushing breath back up

Thoughts will still come
'Am I doing it wrong?'
'When is the bell going to ring?'
Keep doing it
            mind
pushing breath…"

        Hara
                Hara

            above a West Point jet—
          the sky's plummeting
        glass shards not cutting you
                    only projections
    of your mind believing its damaged—
    the fiction and core belief
    our culture is based on—

        Hara

Hara

"I loved your story today
but I'm concerned you cling to it
there's much more
subtle things you may not notice
if you cling to it"

           Hara
                Hara

bodies bodhisattvas compost
smell of fresh dirt
          you are now
             "new compost here"
             "fair to middlin'"
             "ready for the earth"
when you seek deer
   they aren't here
  when you stop looking
         they appear

      *

CHODO'S SELF-PORTRAIT AT STORM KING ART CENTER

"stone wall
        a river"

*

FOR SHUZEN

"WE ARE ALL BROKEN"
a fiction easy to believe
harder to practice
daily sitting

*

SELF-PORTRAITS AT STORM KING ART CENTER

Butterfly needs no runway—
                    my grandfather, ex-
WWII fighter pilot in intensive care ward
            in Belgrade with failing lungs, 7
            pilot lights in The Grail kitchen.

*

And now I'd like to moon
    my good spiritual friends
        walking toward me on the grass
by winding stone wall Goldsworthy and scream
"Self-portrait of the Void! Did you bring your flash?"

"I'd like to see a lifesize picture of
        that not happening

        nothing happening
        like my life."

            *

I don't care about
            your names
                    Sculptors!

    Ikkyu
    take me to
        the moonviewing party
    with saki
    I want to
        love your
    blind Lady Mori with you
        and I'm terrified
            speaking it—
        writing it—
    what's the difference—lines—
    I dried on my lines—peripheral vision black
robes on laundry line—
            an actor stalling

"Listen to the birds"
   the play director said
    and the lines
       appeared in air

"He was teaching you 'bridging,'" said Shuzen
The director was a woman but I didn't say anything
fearing it would be rude
feeling "There's no difference—what—genitalia?"

        Storm King!
        Ah, Storm King.
        Storm King!

               walking in your scorching stunlight
I lost my buddies Michelle and Jeremy.
When The Buddy System breaks down
The Nervous System kicks in!

*

SELF-PORTRAIT AT STORM KING ART CENTER

This map

      makes an ineffective

            and

                fabulously flapping

                      sun hat.

*

ON THE FRONT PORCH OF THE GRAIL

The present a
       seldom
           visited
              country
                  let the

              lines

             go

                where
                  they
                    want to

        unlead by you

           unleaded
                not gasoline
lines in Space
        for grace of all
      sentient beings   OM AH HUM

*

WHEN

when now when with a pen when Zazen
when Kinhin when Dudeman when kin
come to live in an apartment belonging to you
what do you do do you show them in

when when I'm in my bin with tea box
Genine said Chamomile doesn't come
in a box only it's on the lawn

when I strip and shower
when I say the washing gatha

quietly so nobody can hear my—
so embarrassing

when when one syllable
when when is No Mind
when when is not separate from mind

when when is come in when when seed
in   GIN   the juniper berry
I better not drink it even tho
I haven't vowed the precepts

I want to I want to drink GIN
when Now when Now
     when when Now
   Not in Kinhin but now
Give me the Jupiter berry
    I fly to Pluto
    in my Juniper Shuttle
   The atmosphere tastes hot on my lense
 Am I a telescope No No I'm
obnoxious motherfucker mimicking liturgy
when when That's not me when it's me
when can I stay an extra week
when I find a tent when I find
a tent for Sesshin will I find
a tent for Sesshin   is future
not this moment Moment has
Mom in it That's not when
       that's JUDGEMENT

when when will I find out
if I'm really a cosmonaut boyscout
when I skateboard the craters of Jupiter
does Jupiter have craters
    That's the moon
Cute Cute Cute cut it cut it when
Now don't wait for Zazen come in Uji
Uji The Time Being come in
where are you Rodney your buzzcut

I can still see You're gone you left
in a car you were a good roomie
left the light on for me when I was
late for bed lights out when lights out
Lights going down now
                Thunder and Lightning
                  last night
                    didn't obey community silence
                      or lights out
        That's not now that's
              when when when I was this
I was then
 Now I'm when when when when when
  whenny when winter when
          summer when
              spring when

peripheral vision deer
peripheral deer vision
red flakes in spinal August

That was when that was hot when
Kinhin   solar plexus where's that
 are my thumbs in Shashu
   when the solar plexus when the sun
   when the juniper berry orbits
   my gin glass too fast O just
 fast enough

when when one goes
      to Jupiter
          in Juniper Berry
            Shuttle
wave to me when when when
window when window when
window pane when

      *

SENSEI'S ADVICE

"It's none of your business
what you write"
          Thank you
Sensei
    your name is
    a sword
  cutting
   through
   delusion

"The only enemy is delusion."
     —Shurangama Sutra

*

HOW TO TURN "HIDE" INTO "HI"

I was thinking when crickets

       when we were in silence
           just now—
     crickets—
      crickets are not
        giving each other feedback
      not not giving each other feedback
      but communicating with us
      with each other

we're communicating

      with them
      and each other—
         What is there to hide
            Hi!

We're in time   No   we are "The Time Being"
  we are
 going to die
  and dead already

       and
       alive
      together
        now

before we die we have
THIS chance to share
things with each other

                          we are all suffering through and delighting in—
                          is there suffering or delight unique to you—

                                        What is there to hide—
                                               Hi!

       Ikkyu, bless you and Lady Mori
           and the love you are still making
               eight centuries after leaving your bodies

     Thank you
         crickets
    for your
        spontaeneous sutra
delivered to a long oval of folks
   gathered on the front porch
         Summer Ango at The Grail
   thank you crickets for your TORCH

    *

      How would
          we feel
       if the
        crickets
      went mute
tonight
       we
          write
    in
        cricket meter
            tonight
   we write on
      UJI "BEING TIME" UJI

    *

      "Udji" means "Enter", "Come in", "Welcome" in Serbian
      Filip means "Lover of Horses" in Greek
      and yet I am the bad horse the worst horse
      who keeps drinking booze—
      you can't lead me to water
      but I make myself drink
      even though drink
      is pickling my organs—

I am the worst horse
and yet my name means "Lover of Horses"
and to hold that knot in the flame
Zazen is   !

*

   pilot
  lights
stay on—
7 AM in The Grail kitchen—

My grandfather   Milos Marinovic
          a fighter pilot in World War II
                Yugoslavia
                  Britain
                   America—

West Point jet
    cutting up cloud coke
 I don't want coke now I want
to rest and wake up 5:01 AM Rooster Jikido
jump out of nest leaving behind cracked eggs
ring the bell in the ring ring rounds around The Grail house
flapping my arms a titmouse

                Jikido
"If you just swing your arm it rings itself"

ringing the bell
around The Grail house
flapping my arms—

                              Who was I six summers ago?
                              a bat changing shifts
                              with a black swallow.

        *

"Are you staying for the weekend?"
Roshi asked me after we embraced.
        "Yes!"
        "SO...JUST ENJOY"

Wandering the backyard of The Grail house
        hills   sky   branches
                    no "I"
        but The Time Being

            swelling up
                        the backyard packed
            and everything in it
                        a planet
            revolving around
                        one impermanent sun—

the big mind high
         ending
later that night in bed
         when I pray for
Grandfather's health
         and ease is
replaced with empty chest numbness—

         Blessed be these two
         emptinesses, the differences
         between them, and
         the one swelling up they are!

   *

Fugan whispered "NOW!"
at about 10 to 7—
10 minutes before the
two bells to end
morning Zazen and at his
"NOW" I got up (prematurely)
and rang two bells
stood in Gassho with
Kinhin clackers and
waited and everybody got up
"OUTSIDE KINHIN"   CLACK!

*

The Kyosaku ("encouragment stick")
   Koshin whacked me with
     on each shoulder
     when I requested it
     by bowing—
    first Kyosaku hit—
        OW!
        hallway windchimes—
    second Kyosaku
     WHACK!
     WOW!
NOW I'm covered in mud
  from retelling it—
    Sky, clean me off with your Kyosaku
         Lightning!

*

Stop
   looking
      for
         deer
    and
       they
          appear

*

HOW TO FIND A TENT AND EXTEND YOUR RETREAT INTO SESSHIN

Go to Walmart
That way it will go from
    the
 not yet tent
to the tent tent

*

TOKUYU ON PIANO

—Oh, you're the piano player.
                        —I'm   *a*   piano player.
—What a difference an article makes!

*

THE BLACK PAINTINGS

Saturn chomping on Children McNuggets—
ghoul parade through smoking oilwell day—
             sailor
                skull
                     bashed
                            on rocks.
I'm dehydrated, Bach. Water! Water!
No answer.
                    Are you being mean
                    are you a mean being
                    meaning what—

I get up and pour water from a filter pitcher
into Bell Atlantic THE HEART OF COMMUNICATION mug—

       Today my mugshot appears above my head
       I'm wanted in 52 states
                    and especially in
       the 53rd, 54th, and 50 millionth state of
          GEEZE   UNITED STATES
       Really united brain plates in a pyramid
             I eat my dinner with
                    how many lives
                            I.E.D.s

and E.T.s
on movie screens

the drive-in extinct
the human extinct—really?
Is desire? Can desire be extinguished?

The x arms and y legs growing out of me—
I would like to chop them off
but have no cutlery to hand, Bach,

cutting a trail through the Grail Woods
listening to a monk
           chanting a mantra I never
heard before and CRACK!
    the deer run in twos from me—
I stepped on a cracked brown glass bottle—
shards hanging from my ankle I lift ankle
up stop listen to the chant did the glass—
the glass did not
penetrate the skin—let the chant chant you—
Thank you Monk—

A West Point jet BOOMS above us
Roshi says "I'm glad they're so close to us—
reminds us why we're here."
A house full of people in black
vowing to save all sentient beings

succeding failing continuing
to do it anyway—empty ourselves—the consolation of
suchness! no holding on to it
gone with the deer—

I want to run with you deer
through the entire Middle East
bringing peace peace peace
antlers growing up out of
the top of deer's head red deer white spots deer I want
I need you deer do you hear me deer and Bach and
Everybody here not here hearing seeing touching tasting
breathing bleeding
          I won't go to Iraq
          I'm no deer
          The deer is a deer
          I'm me this Bach is
          making a black painting in me
     Goya Goya where did you go
       when your hearing went
       into the pigment of
       what are now called The Black Paintings.

*

wood grain shapes
   on the brown sliding door
     to the piano room
a tall monk
    opening his brown robe
      letting a million children out from it

"Vast is the robe of liberation
A formless field of benefaction
I wear the Tathagata teachings
Saving all sentient beings"

Do you feel a sense of belonging? Well it's time to leave—
      did you get all your belongings together?
    belonging ong ong ong gong gong gong
          gone
     gone all gone way
over top to other shore not leaving one being behind Awakened Mind
      W A H - H O W !

*

SENSEI

attention attending tenderness
please sit me down on that tripod
Zazen

*

LUNCHBREAK WITH SENSEI

"I'm going to the back porch"
said Sensei
    and I followed
  waddling behind her
    a baby penguin.
We sat down to chat at a white wooden table,
I asked her "What's enlightenment?" and she asked
    "Do you think enlightenment
                will change you?"

    "I don't know."

    "No. It won't.
      You know Dido said:

before enlightenment
an asshole
after enlightenment
an asshole"—

and now I'm laughing so hard
I hear a crack
deep in my opening throat
    c h a k r a
and suddenly scared
by my runaway laughter
I stop to ask her
"Is that the pop singer Dido?"
"Oh no, just someone upstate.
I'm going to get some coffee."
I look up at her face

and FLASH
bright green light
shooting through her
smiling and simultaeneously grimacing
skull!
    FLASH   FLASH

Trembling with all the air knocked out of my head
I followed her back to the front porch
where the rest of the sangha was eating and laughing
and sat down dazed
unable to say anything.

Sensei asked the group
if they'd noticed how speeded up
morning Kinhin was becoming.
I had been leading it,
A.M. Jikido tripping on breath.
I tried to respond
"I—

      I—

            I—"
but she kept talking over me
not one of my chopped down I's
could say a thing!

      No-thing!
        Mu!
        Moo!
Now I'm ready for all bodhisattva farmers
    of Upstate New York Chiliocosmos
      to milk my no-cow no-self
        I-less I
        MOO!

nursed on
no-thing!
"Mother is a mirage"
Roshi said tonight
three years later 2010 winter
Being-Time
we sit before her
silent and
she smiles
sensing just when
the room gets tense
cutting through our knots
with her scalpel
laughter!

*

TREE STUMP

Whoever chopped my head off
I like it better this way
now I don't have to carry
all that—

foliage-free!   a crownless tree!   my crown is air I am Sky King
but I make no more oxygen
how selfish of me!
And yet

make your own breathing, I'm tired of it!
I'm ready to be carved into a stupa
for a tired traveller to sit on and rest.
It's no heresy to sit on the stupa Buddha body
I am carved into
as long as you can
say how even
the path of delusion
can lead to Awakening
O Ono no Komachi on the Sotoba!

*

Dear Koshin
thank you for offering to turn the
bedside lamp on
the evening of my Zazen panicattack crying jag
the last hours of my week at the retreat—

"Koshin, can I see Sensei tonight?"

"She sent me, what am I, mashed potatos?"

"You're not mashed potatos, Koshin,
you're a sweet potato!"

"I like sweet potatos!"

"Koshin, my grandfather is dying
I love him more than anybody!"

"Love is pain, Filip.
Death is the great release."

"Yipee!"

"How did you come to Zen?"

"*Zen Flesh Zen Bones*—that fucking book
has been in and out of my life so many times!"

"It's a wonderful book."

"I love it!
            BUT MY MIND IS SO FULL OF ENLIGHTENMENT NARRATIVES
            WHEN DOES IT HAPPEN TO ME?"

    "Should I turn this on?"
you waited for me to nod "Yes" to the lamp
    and turned it on—"Wait, let me cover my eyes to adjust"
        "Me too," and when I turned you said

                "IT'S RIGHT NOW
                        AND IT'S THE HARDEST THING
                        TO PRACTICE"

Koshin   Lamplight

The room begins its illuminated wobble
                                    and stops
a spaceship stalling just before take off—

"But I've had big mind experiences before—
but they stop!"

"Of course they stop, Filip."

"Why?"

        (SIGH)

"Because we can't be only our nose.
We shit and we have livers.

The Dharma takes many forms.
Sometimes grief and anguish
sometimes ecstasy
sometimes cutting up cucumbers.
Whoever clings to the Dharma
defiles the Dharma.

If you know you will go insane
if you stay for Sesshin
and you leave, that's strength.

Knowing your limits is strength.
Take good care of yourself, Filip."

                    *

"O no no no
I'm not here
I'm on holiday!"
said Roshi
when everybody gathered on the front porch
looked up at her
bursting through the screen door
in a swinging black robe
smiling as we were all
ferried together to the other shore.

                    *

"I gotta do a deer check
when I get home."

"What's that?"

"Tick check I meant."

"Deer check—
Any deer around here?"

*

THREE MONTHS LATER IN A MANHATTAN ZENDO LOCKER ROOM

"I can't find my socks—I'm losing things so much these days."

"Me too, I spend most of my time looking for things."

"What's the most interesting thing you've ever lost?"

"My mind. And you?"

"I don't have a reply to that! a thing as interesting as the mind."

*

NUCLEAR FAMILY VOICES IN SEGAKI ("CEREMONY TO RELEASE GHOSTS")

Come ye who have the most vested interest
in my welfare
and
let's see
what
you
have
to
say
about

                                                    how I'm
                                              doing.

           Whoever shows up
                     speak back
                           don't let them
                                  win over
                     you have a role in this
                           too.

                (I am not going to show this to
                                        anyone
                           This is for me alone—

                                        "Good morning, Heartache,
                                        you old gloomy sight…"

—Good morning, Father.

—Oh hello I didn't see you there.
Remember time I made you run
up and down the red stairs while
you were crying from me screaming
at you during math practice?
I didn't know what I was doing.
I am your father doomed to walk the earth
to cross Atlantic from '73 Yugoslavia
to '73 America to land in Pittsburgh

to fly down the dragon's esophagus
in an airplane cooling it with Canada Dry
can in my hand. A-ha! CANADA DRY
GINGERALE—IT'S NOT TOO SWEET AT ALL!
And that dragon has some mean ass
esophagus problems. That dragon's acid
reflux gush burned my hair off I
landed bald in Pittsburgh I came
Coming to America bald—LOOK UP.
You running up and down red staircase.

—Shut up.

—I didn't know what I was doing.
The past is past. Can't do anything about it.
I'm sorry, Son. I'm telling you this on the beach.
Isn't this—aren't you in a forgiving mood.

—Fuck the cock of you that spurted semen out that made me.
Bless the mother's womb that gave birth to me anyway
instinctively forgave your demon semen.

—Demon Semen my favorite soda!
I drank it on the plane coming to America
landing in Pittsburgh, PA.
I poured it on my head, it burned
my hair off.
                    DEMON SEMEN, SODA FOR ME

SODA FOR THEE—
FREE OF CATASTROPHE?—
DRINK ME!

—Strophe means turning point, Father.
This is the turning point where I forgive you.
        No it's not.

                —Oh hello guys.

—Oh, hello Mother.

                —Kitten, leave us alone
                we're talking can't you see we're talking.

—This is the tripod I
        sit on in Zazen
                burning my ass off
        My ass is bald for Speedo Competition
        I'm a high diver in bright blue Speedos
          over Kitchen Beach I dive
           cutting umbilical bunjee cord
                I kiss Paralysis
        it lets go of me No I let go of it
        it falls into a heap
         of black umbrellas   I'm falling
        I'm flying   this wing thing is really great
ARRAY ARRAY ARRAY DOGEN SAY ARRAY

IN MY EAR CUCUMBER ARRAY IN EAR
HEARSAY   I'M HERE TO PLAY FATHER

    —Discipline, Filip!
        Sit down. Where is your mind?
        Clouds are up there.
        You are here. What's 3x2.

—3x2
  equals
fuck you fuck you fuck you—

                —Excuse me did I interrupt
                something?

—No, Mother, just the Oedipal triangle I'm sitting on
        in Zazen
when AM Jikido rings the silver triangle
for sitting it better be on time.
        Oh come on.
        We don't make mistakes.
      Just go on.

           —Did I interrupt something?

—No Mother I love you thanks for coming to pick me up today.

—I haven't picked you up yet.
Shut up and continue
you're on assignment.

—Assignment to where?

—Let's do math.

—Father shut up!

—Canada Semen Dry Gingerale
I shot it into your mother's
womb and out came you!

—No wonder I'm
  Gingerale Head
I used to drink it like crazy
Now I like water
carbonation bothers me
But the incest stick Ha Ha O no
      I made that up arranged it so
                    so what
The insence stick breaks when
      I try to stick it in the center
      of Manjushri travel altar—
   "You are the stick too, breaking"
                said beloved Roshi.
Father, come back here are we still on the beach.

       —Just enjoy yourself, Son.

—Father, I'd rather not I want to talk.

       —We did talk on July 5th, 2007
        You told me all this
        I said then it would be a
        continuing conversation.

—But you're in Belgrade now
 with your dying father
  Yes it's continuing
  CHAIN GENERATIONS
I'd like to take up chain smoking no
   chain breathing no
     just breathing why not just breathing
      slow why not   no?

    —Did I interrupt something?

—Thank you, Mother.

*

nursed on
no-thing!
"Mother is a mirage"
Roshi said tonight
three years later 2010 winter
Being-Time
we sit before her
silent and
she smiles
sensing just when
the room gets tense
cutting through our knots
with her scalpel
laughter!

*

—Thank you, Mother Mirage
Father Mirage Filip Mirage Master
Mirage Mirage Mirage—

—Did I interrupt something?

—Thank you, Mother and Father
Roshi and Sensei
Sangha and sangha—

In Gassho, ("Hands joined together as in prayer, for greeting, please, thank you")

Jikido ("Person who keeps time and cleans the Zendo"
wakes up at five AM before everybody else
walks down the steps
lights candles in the Buddha Hall
drinks a cup of coffee
and walks around the house ringing a bell
which rings itself

2007 / 2010